This Pet Sitter Journal Belongs To:

CLIENT *Information*

NAME:

ADDRESS;

PHONE:

ALTERNATE PHONE:

EMERGENCY CONTACT:

EMAIL;

NOTES:

PET Profile

NAME:

BREED:

AGE:

GENDER:

COAT COLOR:

EYE COLOR:

FAVORITE TOYS:

MEDICAL CONDITIONS:

PET Profile

NAME:

BREED:

AGE:

GENDER:

COAT COLOR:

EYE COLOR:

FAVORITE TOYS:

MEDICAL CONDITIONS:

PET Profile

NAME:

BREED:

AGE:

GENDER:

COAT COLOR:

EYE COLOR:

FAVORITE TOYS:

MEDICAL CONDITIONS:

Vet Information

NAME/BUSINESS:

PHONE:

EMAIL:

ADDRESS:

ADDITIONAL NOTES:

PET SITTER *Notes*
- RESPONSIBILITIES -

	M	T	W	T	F	S	S

PET SITTER *Notes*

- RESPONSIBILITIES -

	M	T	W	T	F	S	S

WEEKLY PET *Journal*

WEEK OF: _____

MONDAY	TUESDAY	WEDNESDAY

THURSDAY	FRIDAY	SATURDAY

SUNDAY	WEEKLY NOTES

WEEKLY PET *Journal*

WEEK OF: ....

MONDAY	TUESDAY	WEDNESDAY

THURSDAY	FRIDAY	SATURDAY

SUNDAY	WEEKLY NOTES

CLIENT *Information*

NAME:

ADDRESS;

PHONE:

ALTERNATE PHONE:

EMERGENCY CONTACT:

EMAIL;

NOTES:

PET Profile

NAME:

BREED:

AGE:

GENDER:

COAT COLOR:

EYE COLOR:

FAVORITE TOYS:

MEDICAL CONDITIONS:

PET Profile

NAME:

BREED:

AGE:

GENDER:

COAT COLOR:

EYE COLOR:

FAVORITE TOYS:

MEDICAL CONDITIONS:

PET Profile

NAME:

BREED:

AGE:

GENDER:

COAT COLOR:

EYE COLOR:

FAVORITE TOYS:

MEDICAL CONDITIONS:

Vet Information

NAME/BUSINESS:

PHONE:

EMAIL:

ADDRESS:

ADDITIONAL NOTES:

PET SITTER *Notes*
- RESPONSIBILITIES -

	M	T	W	T	F	S	S

PET SITTER *Notes*

- RESPONSIBILITIES -

	M	T	W	T	F	S	S

WEEKLY PET *Journal*

WEEK OF: _____

MONDAY	TUESDAY	WEDNESDAY

THURSDAY	FRIDAY	SATURDAY

SUNDAY	WEEKLY NOTES

WEEKLY PET *Journal*

WEEK OF: _____

MONDAY

TUESDAY

WEDNESDAY

THURSDAY

FRIDAY

SATURDAY

SUNDAY

WEEKLY NOTES

CLIENT *Information*

NAME:

ADDRESS;

PHONE:

ALTERNATE PHONE:

EMERGENCY CONTACT:

EMAIL;

NOTES:

PET Profile

NAME: COAT COLOR:

BREED: EYE COLOR:

AGE: FAVORITE TOYS:

GENDER: MEDICAL CONDITIONS:

PET Profile

NAME: COAT COLOR:

BREED: EYE COLOR:

AGE: FAVORITE TOYS:

GENDER: MEDICAL CONDITIONS:

PET Profile

NAME: COAT COLOR:

BREED: EYE COLOR:

AGE: FAVORITE TOYS:

GENDER: MEDICAL CONDITIONS:

Vet Information

NAME/BUSINESS:

PHONE:

EMAIL:

ADDRESS:

ADDITIONAL NOTES:

PET SITTER *Notes*
- RESPONSIBILITIES -

	M	T	W	T	F	S	S

PET SITTER *Notes*

- RESPONSIBILITIES -

	M	T	W	T	F	S	S

WEEKLY PET *Journal*

WEEK OF: _____

MONDAY	TUESDAY	WEDNESDAY

THURSDAY	FRIDAY	SATURDAY

SUNDAY	WEEKLY NOTES

WEEKLY PET *Journal*

WEEK OF: _____

MONDAY	TUESDAY	WEDNESDAY

THURSDAY	FRIDAY	SATURDAY

SUNDAY	WEEKLY NOTES

CLIENT Information

NAME:

ADDRESS;

PHONE:

ALTERNATE PHONE:

EMERGENCY CONTACT:

EMAIL;

NOTES:

PET Profile

NAME: ....

BREED: ....

AGE: ....

GENDER: ....

COAT COLOR: ....

EYE COLOR: ....

FAVORITE TOYS: ....

MEDICAL CONDITIONS: ....

PET Profile

NAME: ....

BREED: ....

AGE: ....

GENDER: ....

COAT COLOR: ....

EYE COLOR: ....

FAVORITE TOYS: ....

MEDICAL CONDITIONS: ....

PET Profile

NAME: ....

BREED: ....

AGE: ....

GENDER: ....

COAT COLOR: ....

EYE COLOR: ....

FAVORITE TOYS: ....

MEDICAL CONDITIONS: ....

Vet Information

NAME/BUSINESS:

PHONE:

EMAIL:

ADDRESS:

ADDITIONAL NOTES:

PET SITTER *Notes*
- RESPONSIBILITIES -

	M	T	W	T	F	S	S

PET SITTER *Notes*
- RESPONSIBILITIES -

	M	T	W	T	F	S	S

WEEKLY PET *Journal*

WEEK OF:

MONDAY

TUESDAY

WEDNESDAY

THURSDAY

FRIDAY

SATURDAY

SUNDAY

WEEKLY NOTES

WEEKLY PET *Journal*

WEEK OF: _____

| MONDAY | TUESDAY | WEDNESDAY |

| THURSDAY | FRIDAY | SATURDAY |

| SUNDAY | WEEKLY NOTES |

CLIENT *Information*

NAME:

ADDRESS;

PHONE:

ALTERNATE PHONE:

EMERGENCY CONTACT:

EMAIL;

NOTES:

PET Profile

NAME:

COAT COLOR:

BREED:

EYE COLOR:

AGE:

FAVORITE TOYS:

GENDER:

MEDICAL CONDITIONS:

PET Profile

NAME:

COAT COLOR:

BREED:

EYE COLOR:

AGE:

FAVORITE TOYS:

GENDER:

MEDICAL CONDITIONS:

PET Profile

NAME:

COAT COLOR:

BREED:

EYE COLOR:

AGE:

FAVORITE TOYS:

GENDER:

MEDICAL CONDITIONS:

Vet Information

NAME/BUSINESS:

PHONE:

EMAIL:

ADDRESS:

ADDITIONAL NOTES:

PET SITTER *Notes*
- RESPONSIBILITIES -

	M	T	W	T	F	S	S

PET SITTER *Notes*

- RESPONSIBILITIES -

	M	T	W	T	F	S	S

WEEKLY PET *Journal*

WEEK OF: _____

MONDAY	TUESDAY	WEDNESDAY

THURSDAY	FRIDAY	SATURDAY

SUNDAY	WEEKLY NOTES

WEEKLY PET *Journal*

WEEK OF: _____

MONDAY	TUESDAY	WEDNESDAY

THURSDAY	FRIDAY	SATURDAY

SUNDAY	WEEKLY NOTES

CLIENT *Information*

NAME:

ADDRESS;

PHONE:

ALTERNATE PHONE:

EMERGENCY CONTACT:

EMAIL;

NOTES:

PET Profile

NAME: _____

BREED: _____

AGE: _____

GENDER: _____

COAT COLOR: _____

EYE COLOR: _____

FAVORITE TOYS: _____

MEDICAL CONDITIONS: _____

PET Profile

NAME: _____

BREED: _____

AGE: _____

GENDER: _____

COAT COLOR: _____

EYE COLOR: _____

FAVORITE TOYS: _____

MEDICAL CONDITIONS: _____

PET Profile

NAME: _____

BREED: _____

AGE: _____

GENDER: _____

COAT COLOR: _____

EYE COLOR: _____

FAVORITE TOYS: _____

MEDICAL CONDITIONS: _____

Vet Information

NAME/BUSINESS:

PHONE:

EMAIL:

ADDRESS:

ADDITIONAL NOTES:

PET SITTER *Notes*
- RESPONSIBILITIES -

	M	T	W	T	F	S	S

PET SITTER *Notes*
- RESPONSIBILITIES -

	M	T	W	T	F	S	S

WEEKLY PET *Journal*

WEEK OF: _____

MONDAY	TUESDAY	WEDNESDAY

THURSDAY	FRIDAY	SATURDAY

SUNDAY	WEEKLY NOTES

WEEKLY PET *Journal*

WEEK OF: _____

MONDAY	TUESDAY	WEDNESDAY

THURSDAY	FRIDAY	SATURDAY

SUNDAY	WEEKLY NOTES

CLIENT Information

NAME:

ADDRESS;

PHONE:

ALTERNATE PHONE:

EMERGENCY CONTACT:

EMAIL;

NOTES:

PET Profile

NAME:

BREED:

AGE:

GENDER:

COAT COLOR:

EYE COLOR:

FAVORITE TOYS:

MEDICAL CONDITIONS:

PET Profile

NAME:

BREED:

AGE:

GENDER:

COAT COLOR:

EYE COLOR:

FAVORITE TOYS:

MEDICAL CONDITIONS:

PET Profile

NAME:

BREED:

AGE:

GENDER:

COAT COLOR:

EYE COLOR:

FAVORITE TOYS:

MEDICAL CONDITIONS:

Vet Information

NAME/BUSINESS:

PHONE:

EMAIL:

ADDRESS:

ADDITIONAL NOTES:

PET SITTER *Notes*
- RESPONSIBILITIES -

	M	T	W	T	F	S	S

PET SITTER *Notes*

- RESPONSIBILITIES -

	M	T	W	T	F	S	S

WEEKLY PET *Journal*

WEEK OF: _____

MONDAY	TUESDAY	WEDNESDAY

THURSDAY	FRIDAY	SATURDAY

SUNDAY	WEEKLY NOTES

WEEKLY PET *Journal*

WEEK OF: _____

MONDAY	TUESDAY	WEDNESDAY

THURSDAY	FRIDAY	SATURDAY

SUNDAY	WEEKLY NOTES

CLIENT *Information*

NAME:

ADDRESS;

PHONE:

ALTERNATE PHONE:

EMERGENCY CONTACT:

EMAIL;

NOTES:

PET Profile

NAME:

COAT COLOR:

BREED:

EYE COLOR:

AGE:

FAVORITE TOYS:

GENDER:

MEDICAL CONDITIONS:

PET Profile

NAME:

COAT COLOR:

BREED:

EYE COLOR:

AGE:

FAVORITE TOYS:

GENDER:

MEDICAL CONDITIONS:

PET Profile

NAME:

COAT COLOR:

BREED:

EYE COLOR:

AGE:

FAVORITE TOYS:

GENDER:

MEDICAL CONDITIONS:

Vet Information

NAME/BUSINESS:

PHONE:

EMAIL:

ADDRESS:

ADDITIONAL NOTES:

PET SITTER *Notes*
- RESPONSIBILITIES -

	M	T	W	T	F	S	S

PET SITTER Notes

- RESPONSIBILITIES -

	M	T	W	T	F	S	S

WEEKLY PET *Journal*

WEEK OF: _____

MONDAY	TUESDAY	WEDNESDAY

THURSDAY	FRIDAY	SATURDAY

SUNDAY	WEEKLY NOTES

WEEKLY PET *Journal*

WEEK OF: _____

MONDAY	TUESDAY	WEDNESDAY

THURSDAY	FRIDAY	SATURDAY

SUNDAY	WEEKLY NOTES

CLIENT Information

NAME:

ADDRESS;

PHONE:

ALTERNATE PHONE:

EMERGENCY CONTACT:

EMAIL;

NOTES:

PET Profile

NAME:

COAT COLOR:

BREED:

EYE COLOR:

AGE:

FAVORITE TOYS:

GENDER:

MEDICAL CONDITIONS:

PET Profile

NAME:

COAT COLOR:

BREED:

EYE COLOR:

AGE:

FAVORITE TOYS:

GENDER:

MEDICAL CONDITIONS:

PET Profile

NAME:

COAT COLOR:

BREED:

EYE COLOR:

AGE:

FAVORITE TOYS:

GENDER:

MEDICAL CONDITIONS:

Vet Information

NAME/BUSINESS:

PHONE:

EMAIL:

ADDRESS:

ADDITIONAL NOTES:

PET SITTER *Notes*
- RESPONSIBILITIES -

	M	T	W	T	F	S	S

PET SITTER *Notes*

- RESPONSIBILITIES -

	M	T	W	T	F	S	S

WEEKLY PET *Journal*

WEEK OF: _____

MONDAY	TUESDAY	WEDNESDAY

THURSDAY	FRIDAY	SATURDAY

SUNDAY	WEEKLY NOTES

WEEKLY PET *Journal*

WEEK OF: _____

MONDAY

TUESDAY

WEDNESDAY

THURSDAY

FRIDAY

SATURDAY

SUNDAY

WEEKLY NOTES

CLIENT *Information*

NAME:

ADDRESS;

PHONE:

ALTERNATE PHONE:

EMERGENCY CONTACT:

EMAIL;

NOTES:

PET *Profile*

NAME:

COAT COLOR:

BREED:

EYE COLOR:

AGE:

FAVORITE TOYS:

GENDER:

MEDICAL CONDITIONS:

PET *Profile*

NAME:

COAT COLOR:

BREED:

EYE COLOR:

AGE:

FAVORITE TOYS:

GENDER:

MEDICAL CONDITIONS:

PET *Profile*

NAME:

COAT COLOR:

BREED:

EYE COLOR:

AGE:

FAVORITE TOYS:

GENDER:

MEDICAL CONDITIONS:

Vet Information

NAME/BUSINESS:

PHONE:

EMAIL:

ADDRESS:

ADDITIONAL NOTES:

PET SITTER *Notes*
- RESPONSIBILITIES -

	M	T	W	T	F	S	S

PET SITTER *Notes*
- RESPONSIBILITIES -

	M	T	W	T	F	S	S

WEEKLY PET *Journal*

WEEK OF: _____

MONDAY	TUESDAY	WEDNESDAY

THURSDAY	FRIDAY	SATURDAY

SUNDAY	WEEKLY NOTES

WEEKLY PET *Journal*

WEEK OF: _____

MONDAY	TUESDAY	WEDNESDAY

THURSDAY	FRIDAY	SATURDAY

SUNDAY	WEEKLY NOTES

CLIENT *Information*

NAME:

ADDRESS;

PHONE:

ALTERNATE PHONE:

EMERGENCY CONTACT:

EMAIL;

NOTES:

PET *Profile*

NAME:

BREED:

AGE:

GENDER:

COAT COLOR:

EYE COLOR:

FAVORITE TOYS:

MEDICAL CONDITIONS:

PET *Profile*

NAME:

BREED:

AGE:

GENDER:

COAT COLOR:

EYE COLOR:

FAVORITE TOYS:

MEDICAL CONDITIONS:

PET *Profile*

NAME:

BREED:

AGE:

GENDER:

COAT COLOR:

EYE COLOR:

FAVORITE TOYS:

MEDICAL CONDITIONS:

Vet Information

NAME/BUSINESS:

PHONE:

EMAIL:

ADDRESS:

ADDITIONAL NOTES:

PET SITTER Notes
- RESPONSIBILITIES -

	M	T	W	T	F	S	S

PET SITTER *Notes*
- RESPONSIBILITIES -

	M	T	W	T	F	S	S

WEEKLY PET *Journal*

WEEK OF: _____

MONDAY

TUESDAY

WEDNESDAY

THURSDAY

FRIDAY

SATURDAY

SUNDAY

WEEKLY NOTES

WEEKLY PET *Journal*

WEEK OF: _____

MONDAY	TUESDAY	WEDNESDAY

THURSDAY	FRIDAY	SATURDAY

SUNDAY	WEEKLY NOTES

CLIENT *Information*

NAME:

ADDRESS;

PHONE:

ALTERNATE PHONE:

EMERGENCY CONTACT:

EMAIL;

NOTES:

PET Profile

NAME: COAT COLOR:

BREED: EYE COLOR:

AGE: FAVORITE TOYS:

GENDER: MEDICAL CONDITIONS:

PET Profile

NAME: COAT COLOR:

BREED: EYE COLOR:

AGE: FAVORITE TOYS:

GENDER: MEDICAL CONDITIONS:

PET Profile

NAME: COAT COLOR:

BREED: EYE COLOR:

AGE: FAVORITE TOYS:

GENDER: MEDICAL CONDITIONS:

Vet Information

NAME/BUSINESS:

PHONE:

EMAIL:

ADDRESS:

ADDITIONAL NOTES:

PET SITTER Notes

- RESPONSIBILITIES -

	M	T	W	T	F	S	S

PET SITTER *Notes*

- RESPONSIBILITIES -

	M	T	W	T	F	S	S

WEEKLY PET *Journal*

WEEK OF: _____

MONDAY	TUESDAY	WEDNESDAY

THURSDAY	FRIDAY	SATURDAY

SUNDAY	WEEKLY NOTES

WEEKLY PET *Journal*

WEEK OF: _____

MONDAY	TUESDAY	WEDNESDAY

THURSDAY	FRIDAY	SATURDAY

SUNDAY	WEEKLY NOTES

CLIENT *Information*

NAME:

ADDRESS;

PHONE:

ALTERNATE PHONE:

EMERGENCY CONTACT:

EMAIL;

NOTES:

PET Profile

NAME:

BREED:

AGE:

GENDER:

COAT COLOR:

EYE COLOR:

FAVORITE TOYS:

MEDICAL CONDITIONS:

PET Profile

NAME:

BREED:

AGE:

GENDER:

COAT COLOR:

EYE COLOR:

FAVORITE TOYS:

MEDICAL CONDITIONS:

PET Profile

NAME:

BREED:

AGE:

GENDER:

COAT COLOR:

EYE COLOR:

FAVORITE TOYS:

MEDICAL CONDITIONS:

Vet Information

NAME/BUSINESS:

PHONE:

EMAIL:

ADDRESS:

ADDITIONAL NOTES:

PET SITTER *Notes*

- RESPONSIBILITIES -

	M	T	W	T	F	S	S

PET SITTER *Notes*
- RESPONSIBILITIES -

	M	T	W	T	F	S	S

WEEKLY PET *Journal*

WEEK OF: _____

MONDAY	TUESDAY	WEDNESDAY

THURSDAY	FRIDAY	SATURDAY

SUNDAY	WEEKLY NOTES

WEEKLY PET *Journal*

WEEK OF: _____

MONDAY	TUESDAY	WEDNESDAY

THURSDAY	FRIDAY	SATURDAY

SUNDAY	WEEKLY NOTES

CLIENT *Information*

NAME:

ADDRESS;

PHONE:

ALTERNATE PHONE:

EMERGENCY CONTACT:

EMAIL;

NOTES:

PET Profile

NAME: ....

BREED: ....

AGE: ....

GENDER: ....

COAT COLOR: ....

EYE COLOR: ....

FAVORITE TOYS: ....

MEDICAL CONDITIONS: ....

PET Profile

NAME: ....

BREED: ....

AGE: ....

GENDER: ....

COAT COLOR: ....

EYE COLOR: ....

FAVORITE TOYS: ....

MEDICAL CONDITIONS: ....

PET Profile

NAME: ....

BREED: ....

AGE: ....

GENDER: ....

COAT COLOR: ....

EYE COLOR: ....

FAVORITE TOYS: ....

MEDICAL CONDITIONS: ....

Vet Information

NAME/BUSINESS:

PHONE:

EMAIL:

ADDRESS:

ADDITIONAL NOTES:

PET SITTER *Notes*
- RESPONSIBILITIES -

	M	T	W	T	F	S	S

PET SITTER *Notes*
- RESPONSIBILITIES -

	M	T	W	T	F	S	S

WEEKLY PET *Journal*

WEEK OF: _____

MONDAY	TUESDAY	WEDNESDAY

THURSDAY	FRIDAY	SATURDAY

SUNDAY	WEEKLY NOTES

WEEKLY PET *Journal*

WEEK OF: _____

MONDAY	TUESDAY	WEDNESDAY

THURSDAY	FRIDAY	SATURDAY

SUNDAY	WEEKLY NOTES

CLIENT *Information*

NAME:

ADDRESS;

PHONE:

ALTERNATE PHONE:

EMERGENCY CONTACT:

EMAIL;

NOTES:

PET Profile

NAME:

BREED:

AGE:

GENDER:

COAT COLOR:

EYE COLOR:

FAVORITE TOYS:

MEDICAL CONDITIONS:

PET Profile

NAME:

BREED:

AGE:

GENDER:

COAT COLOR:

EYE COLOR:

FAVORITE TOYS:

MEDICAL CONDITIONS:

PET Profile

NAME:

BREED:

AGE:

GENDER:

COAT COLOR:

EYE COLOR:

FAVORITE TOYS:

MEDICAL CONDITIONS:

Vet Information

NAME/BUSINESS:

PHONE:

EMAIL:

ADDRESS:

ADDITIONAL NOTES:

PET SITTER *Notes*
- RESPONSIBILITIES -

	M	T	W	T	F	S	S

PET SITTER *Notes*
- RESPONSIBILITIES -

	M	T	W	T	F	S	S

WEEKLY PET *Journal*

WEEK OF: _____

MONDAY	TUESDAY	WEDNESDAY

THURSDAY	FRIDAY	SATURDAY

SUNDAY	WEEKLY NOTES

WEEKLY PET *Journal*

WEEK OF: _____

MONDAY	TUESDAY	WEDNESDAY

THURSDAY	FRIDAY	SATURDAY

SUNDAY	WEEKLY NOTES

CLIENT *Information*

NAME:

ADDRESS;

PHONE:

ALTERNATE PHONE:

EMERGENCY CONTACT:

EMAIL;

NOTES:

PET Profile

NAME:

BREED:

AGE:

GENDER:

COAT COLOR:

EYE COLOR:

FAVORITE TOYS:

MEDICAL CONDITIONS:

PET Profile

NAME:

BREED:

AGE:

GENDER:

COAT COLOR:

EYE COLOR:

FAVORITE TOYS:

MEDICAL CONDITIONS:

PET Profile

NAME:

BREED:

AGE:

GENDER:

COAT COLOR:

EYE COLOR:

FAVORITE TOYS:

MEDICAL CONDITIONS:

Vet Information

NAME/BUSINESS:

PHONE:

EMAIL:

ADDRESS:

ADDITIONAL NOTES:

PET SITTER *Notes*
- RESPONSIBILITIES -

	M	T	W	T	F	S	S

PET SITTER *Notes*
- RESPONSIBILITIES -

	M	T	W	T	F	S	S

WEEKLY PET *Journal*

WEEK OF: ....

MONDAY	TUESDAY	WEDNESDAY

THURSDAY	FRIDAY	SATURDAY

SUNDAY	WEEKLY NOTES

WEEKLY PET *Journal*

WEEK OF: _____

MONDAY	TUESDAY	WEDNESDAY

THURSDAY	FRIDAY	SATURDAY

SUNDAY	WEEKLY NOTES

CLIENT *Information*

NAME:

ADDRESS;

PHONE:

ALTERNATE PHONE:

EMERGENCY CONTACT:

EMAIL;

NOTES:

PET *Profile*

NAME:

BREED:

AGE:

GENDER:

COAT COLOR:

EYE COLOR:

FAVORITE TOYS:

MEDICAL CONDITIONS:

PET *Profile*

NAME:

BREED:

AGE:

GENDER:

COAT COLOR:

EYE COLOR:

FAVORITE TOYS:

MEDICAL CONDITIONS:

PET *Profile*

NAME:

BREED:

AGE:

GENDER:

COAT COLOR:

EYE COLOR:

FAVORITE TOYS:

MEDICAL CONDITIONS:

Vet Information

NAME/BUSINESS:

PHONE:

EMAIL:

ADDRESS:

ADDITIONAL NOTES:

PET SITTER *Notes*
- RESPONSIBILITIES -

	M	T	W	T	F	S	S

PET SITTER *Notes*
- RESPONSIBILITIES -

	M	T	W	T	F	S	S

WEEKLY PET *Journal*

WEEK OF: _____

MONDAY	TUESDAY	WEDNESDAY

THURSDAY	FRIDAY	SATURDAY

SUNDAY	WEEKLY NOTES

WEEKLY PET *Journal*

WEEK OF: _____

MONDAY	TUESDAY	WEDNESDAY

THURSDAY	FRIDAY	SATURDAY

SUNDAY	WEEKLY NOTES

Made in the USA
Las Vegas, NV
28 November 2020